The Countries

Mexico

Kate A. Furlong
ABDO Publishing Company

visit us at
www.abdopub.com

Published by ABDO Publishing Company, 4940 Viking Drive, Suite 622, Edina, Minnesota 55435. Copyright © 2000 Abdo Consulting Group, Inc., Pentagon Tower, P.O. Box 36036, Minneapolis, Minnesota 55435 USA. International copyrights reserved in all countries. No part of this book may be reproduced in any form without written permission from the publisher.

Printed in the United States.

Interior Photos: AP Wideworld Photos, Corbis
Editors: Bob Italia and Tamara L. Britton
Art Direction & Maps: Pat Laurel

Library of Congress Cataloging-in-Publication Data

Furlong, Kate A., 1977-
   Mexico / Kate A. Furlong.
      p. cm. -- (The Countries)
Includes index.
Summary: An introduction to the geography, history, culture, and people of Mexico.
ISBN 1-57765-390-4
  1. Mexico--Juvenile literature. [1. Mexico.] I. Title. II. Series.

F1208.5 .F87 2000
972

                                      00-026671

Contents

Y-29-02

¡Hola!

In Mexico, people say *hola* (hello) to greet each other. They live in the most northern country in **Latin America**. It is a land of deserts, mountains, beaches, and tropical rain forests. These areas are home to many unusual plants and animals.

Most Mexicans are part Indian and part Spanish. They have created a society with its own special style of music, food, festivals, and art.

Mexicans have worked hard to improve their **economy**. Their land provides them with vast supplies of oil and **minerals**. Mexico's beautiful beaches draw thousands of **tourists**. And people manufacture goods and farm the land.

Many Mexicans live in large cities. Mexico's capital is the largest city in the world. Mexican cities have parks, universities, and museums. They also have important **industries**.

The Mexican government is a republic. It follows a **constitution** that tries to improve the lives of all Mexicans. The head of the Mexican government is the president. Mexicans elect him or her.

During its history, Mexico has been home to ancient Indian civilizations and European explorers. Today, it is a modern nation of more than 100 million people. It is rich in people, history, and culture.

A Mexican boy leans against a pile of serapes at a Cancún market. A serape is a colorful woolen shawl worn over the shoulders.

Fast Facts

OFFICIAL NAME: United Mexican States
(Estados Unidos Mexicanos)
CAPITAL: Mexico City

LAND
- Mountain Ranges: Sierra Madre Occidental, Sierra Madre Oriental, Sierra Madre del Sur
- Highest Point: Volcán Citlaltépetl (18,700 feet; 5,700 meters)
- Major Rivers: Río Bravo del Norte, Río Lerma

PEOPLE
- Population: 100,294,036 (1999 est.)
- Major Cities: Mexico City, Guadalajara, Monterrey
- Official Language: Spanish
- Religion: Roman Catholicism (no official religion)

GOVERNMENT
- Form: Federal Republic
- Head: President
- Legislature: Congress (made up of the Senate and the Chamber of Deputies)
- Flag: Green, white, and red with the coat of arms in the center
- Other Symbols: Coat of arms (an eagle sitting on a cactus while eating a snake)
- Nationhood: 1821

ECONOMY
- Agricultural Products: corn, coffee, sugarcane, tomatoes, bananas, wheat, sorghum, barley, rice, beans, potatoes, cacao
- Mining Products: petroleum, natural gas, zinc, salt, silver, copper
- Manufactured Products: motor vehicles, processed foods, beverages, iron and steel, chemicals, electrical machinery
- Money: Peso (one hundred centavos equal one peso)

Mexico's Flag

2000 Peso bill

Timeline

9,000 B.C.	Early American Indians settle in Mexico
A.D. 250-900	Height of Mayan Empire
1325	Aztecs build Tenochtitlán
1517	Spanish explorers arrive in present-day Mexico
1521	Spanish explorers conquer Aztec Empire and make Mexico a Spanish colony
1810	Father Miguel Hidalgo y Costilla's call leads to war of independence with Spain
1821	Mexico gains independence from Spain
1846	Mexican War with U.S. begins
1848	Mexican War ends
1863	French seize control of Mexico
1867	Mexico gains independence from France
1876	Porfirio Díaz takes control of Mexico
1910	Mexican Revolution
1917	Mexicans write the Constitution of 1917
1942	Mexico becomes active in World War II
1976	Large oil deposits found in Tabasco and Chiapas
1985	Powerful earthquake damages Mexico City
1993	Mexico, Canada, and U.S. create NAFTA

Ancient People, Modern Nation

Around 9,000 B.C., early American Indians became the first people to live in Mexico. They formed many societies. Some of these societies grew into great empires. The Mayan and Aztec Empires were the most advanced.

The Maya lived in Mexico's Yucatán **Peninsula** and parts of Central America. They built large stone cities and temples. They also created a writing system and a calendar. And they studied astronomy and mathematics. The Maya flourished between A.D. 250 and 900. Then their empire crumbled for unknown reasons.

The Aztecs were another important Mexican civilization. They lived in present-day Mexico City. Agriculture, religion, and a

Scientists think the Maya built El Caracol to study astronomy.

strong army were important to the Aztecs. In 1325, they built a powerful city called Tenochtitlán. It was built on an island in Lake Texcoco. The Aztec Empire ruled from the 1300s until the Spaniards arrived.

In 1517, Spanish explorers traveled to present-day Mexico. They wanted to claim the land for King Charles I of Spain. The Spaniards and the Aztecs fought for control of the land. Hernán Cortés led the Spaniards to victory over the Aztecs in 1521.

Soon after, the Spaniards established a colony called New Spain. They built cities, churches, and large farms called haciendas. The Spaniards forced the Indians to work for them, and pay special taxes called tributes. The Catholic Church had much power over the colony. It forced the Indians to give up their religion.

Hernán Cortés with Aztec leader Montezuma II

New Spain remained a colony for three hundred years. But the people of New Spain wanted to be independent. On September 16, 1810, Father Miguel Hidalgo y Costilla called for a revolt against Spain. His call started a war of independence.

The people of New Spain fought the Spaniards for eleven years. In 1821, Mexico finally won its independence and formed a republic.

Soon, Mexico faced problems. The U.S. and Mexico disagreed on Texas's southern border. And the U.S. wanted to buy California from Mexico. But Mexico did not want to sell it.

In 1846, the U.S. and Mexico went to war. The Mexican War ended two years later. The U.S. received a large section of Mexican land.

In 1847, the U.S. won the Battle of Buena Vista in the Mexican War. This victory gave the U.S. control of northern Mexico.

Mexicans were upset with America's easy victory in the Mexican War. Benito Juárez and others tried to **reform** Mexico. They wanted to reduce the Catholic Church's power, improve the **economy**, and create a legal system of justice. There were many people against this movement. It caused a civil war. But Juárez and his followers won.

This was a time of great political and economic disorder in Mexico. France took advantage of Mexico's weak state. In 1863, France seized control of Mexico. France ruled Mexico for four years.

Porfirio Díaz

In 1876, Porfirio Díaz established order in Mexico. Díaz ruled Mexico for thirty-five years. He made great efforts to make Mexico more modern. But the people felt Díaz took advantage of **rural** Mexicans, Indians, and city workers who had no rights.

In 1910, Mexicans called for a **revolution**. Emiliano Zapata and Francisco "Pancho" Villa led revolutionary groups. They demanded land **reform**, workers' rights, and improved education. Díaz stepped down in 1911. In 1917, a new **constitution** was written. It granted most of the revolutionaries' demands.

General Emiliano Zapata

The Mexican government worked hard to put its new constitution into practice. The government built thousands of new schools across the country. It supported a national workers' **union**. And it gave land to peasants.

In 1942, Mexico became active in **World War II**. Its troops saw little action. But the country supplied the U.S. with many important raw materials.

General Pancho Villa leads a rebel group in the Mexican Revolution.

After **World War II**, Mexico grew at an amazing rate. The population increased greatly. And the **economy** prospered. In 1976, Mexicans discovered huge oil fields near Tabasco and Chiapas. Selling this oil made up a large part of Mexico's economy.

In the 1980s, Mexico faced problems. Oil prices dropped. Mexico owed other countries much money. Many Mexicans could not find jobs. And illegal drugs from Mexico entered the U.S. This hurt relations between the two countries.

In 1993, Mexico formed the North American Free Trade Agreement (NAFTA) with Canada and the U.S. It brought many new jobs to Mexico.

Today, Mexicans are still working hard to build their **industry** and strengthen their economy. They are also trying to improve their political system. With these changes, Mexicans hope to create an even stronger nation.

Jobs created by NAFTA have improved Mexico's economy.

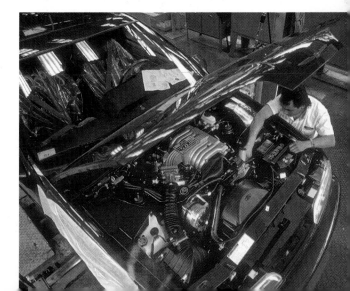

Plateaus & Peninsulas

Mexico is in North America. It is south of the United States and north of Guatemala and Belize. The Gulf of Mexico and the Caribbean Sea form Mexico's eastern border. The Pacific Ocean borders Mexico on the west.

Mexico has two major **peninsulas**. The Yucatán Peninsula is in southern Mexico near Belize. The Baja California Peninsula is on Mexico's western side, just south of California.

Mexico has three major mountain ranges. The Sierra Madre Occidental runs along western Mexico. The Sierra Madre del Sur runs along the southern shore. The Sierra Madre Oriental is on Mexico's eastern side. Streams have carved deep canyons into the Sierra Madre Oriental. The largest is the Copper Canyon.

Copper Canyon

Between the Sierra Madre Oriental and the Sierra Madre Occidental lies the Mexican **Plateau**. Most Mexicans live in this area.

Southern Mexico often has **earthquakes**. In 1985, a powerful earthquake shook Mexico City. It killed about 7,000 people and wrecked many buildings.

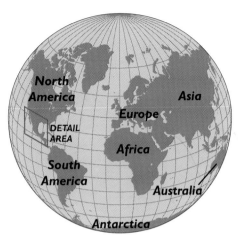

Volcanoes are another danger in southern Mexico. They can spew lava, ash, and steam. Mexico's active volcanoes are Paracutín, El Chichón, Popocatépetl, and Colima. Volcán Citlaltépetl, Mexico's highest peak, is **dormant**.

Mexico has few rivers and lakes. The largest river is the Río Bravo del Norte. It is called the Río Grande in the U.S. It forms part of the border between the U.S. and Mexico.

The Río Lerma is Mexico's second-largest river. It flows into Mexico's largest lake, Lake Chapala.

Mexico's climate changes from region to region. The north has hot, dry deserts. The south is tropical. In the tropics, it is warm in the low areas and cooler at higher elevations. Most of Mexico receives little rain.

Colima is one of North America's most active volcanoes.

Southern Mexico's tropical rain forest is home to the Lacandón people. They are descendants of the Maya.

Rainfall

**AVERAGE
YEARLY RAINFALL**

<u>Inches</u>		<u>Centimeters</u>
Under 10		*Under 25*
10 - 20		*25 - 50*
20 - 40		*50 - 100*
40 - 60		*100 - 150*
60 - 80		*150 - 200*
Over 80		*Over 200*

Temperature

Winter

**AVERAGE
TEMPERATURE**

<u>Fahrenheit</u>		<u>Celsius</u>
Over 86°		*Over 30°*
68° - 86°		*20° - 30°*
50° - 68°		*10° - 20°*
32° - 50°		*0° - 10°*

Summer

Plants & Animals

Mexico has a variety of plants and animals because it has so many climates.

Many cactuses grow in northern Mexico's deserts. This area also has **succulents** and desert **scrub plants**. Rabbits, snakes, and armadillos live in the deserts and the flat, treeless areas of northern Mexico. Some of the mountains in this area are home to deer, pumas, and coyotes.

The Mexican **Plateau** has leafy trees and evergreens. But few forests have survived hundreds of years of human settlement. Human settlement also greatly reduced the number of animals on the plateau.

Tropical rain forests cover parts of the Gulf Coast and the Yucatán **Peninsula**. **Ferns**, palm trees, and mosses grow in these areas.

Cactuses and desert scrub plants in northern Mexico

Mexico's tropical rain forests are home to spider monkeys. These monkeys spend almost all their time in the treetops. Their long arms and tails make it easy for them to move quickly between tree branches.

A spider monkey

A jaguar

Jaguars also live in Mexico's tropical rain forests. The jaguar is the largest cat in the Americas. Most jaguars are orange with black spots. They are fast, graceful animals. And they are good swimmers and hunters.

Mexico's rain forests also have many kinds of parrots. Most parrots have strong, hooked beaks. They are usually very colorful. Parrots like to eat seeds, nuts, fruit, and flowers.

The waters surrounding Mexico have lots of animals, too. These waters have **reefs** and brightly-colored fish. And near Baja California, people have spotted the blue whale. It is the world's largest animal.

Two Cultures, One People

Many Spaniards moved to Mexico after it became a colony. Some Spaniards and Indians had children together. The children were part Spanish and part Indian, so they were called *mestizos* (mixed). Today, most Mexicans are *mestizos*.

The Spaniards brought their language to Mexico. Most Mexicans speak Spanish. But some Indian groups still speak their native languages.

The Spaniards also brought the Catholic religion to Mexico. Many Indians converted from their **traditional** religions to Catholicism. Today, Mexico has no official religion. But nearly all Mexicans are Catholic.

Mexico's population is growing quickly. It is made up of many young people. More than a third of Mexicans are under age fifteen.

After school, many young Mexicans like to relax in their city's plaza.

Mexican children must go to school from age six to age fourteen. Then they can go to secondary schools. There, students can learn **technical** skills. Or, they can go to schools that will prepare them for college.

Over the years, Mexico's government has worked hard to improve rural schools.

In Mexico, there is a big difference between social classes. Many people are poor. Only a few are rich. But Mexico's growing **industries** have helped the middle class become larger.

A typical Mexican family is made up of a mother, father, and children. Grandparents are often active in the family. Godparents are also important to Mexican families. They support their godchildren in religious activities.

In parts of Mexico, **traditional** clothing is still worn by some Indians. It is made of cotton and wool with colorful patterns. But western-style clothing like that worn in the U.S. and Canada has become popular.

There are many kinds of homes in Mexico. **Traditional** Indian homes are made from a variety of materials, including thatch, mud, and twigs covered with clay.

Other homes are made of adobe bricks with tiled roofs. City houses are right on the sidewalk. They have bars on the windows. A city house's walls may surround a small outdoor area called a courtyard. In the poorest neighborhoods, houses are made of cardboard, tin, and other scraps.

Each region in Mexico has its own special food. But beans, rice, chili peppers, and tomatoes are common throughout the country. Tortillas are also common. They are a round, flat bread made from corn.

In Mexico, lunch is the largest meal of the day. Usually it is eaten at home. Lunch is followed by a short nap called a *siesta*.

A woman making tortillas

Mexican Hot Chocolate

The Aztecs used crushed **cacao** beans to make a hot, bitter drink. Over time, this grew into the sweet drink known as hot chocolate.

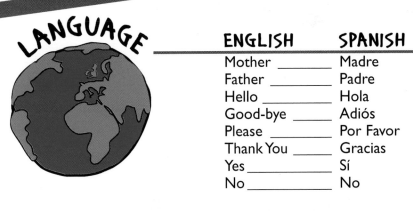

4 oz. sweet baking chocolate
4 cups milk
1 1/2 tbsp. sugar

2 oz. unsweetened chocolate
1 cinnamon stick
1/2 tsp. almond extract

Put both kinds of chocolate in a microwave-safe bowl. Melt the chocolate in the microwave. Set aside. In another microwave-safe bowl, combine the milk and cinnamon stick. Heat the milk mixture in the microwave until hot but not boiling. Combine the melted chocolate and the hot milk mixture. Add the sugar and almond extract. Beat the mixture with a whisk until frothy. Take out the cinnamon stick and serve. This recipe makes four servings.

AN IMPORTANT NOTE TO THE CHEF: Always have an adult help with the preparation and cooking of food. Never use kitchen utensils or appliances without adult permission and supervision.

LANGUAGE

ENGLISH	SPANISH
Mother _____	Madre
Father _____	Padre
Hello _____	Hola
Good-bye _____	Adiós
Please _____	Por Favor
Thank You _____	Gracias
Yes _____	Sí
No _____	No

Economy

Oil, **mining**, **tourism**, manufacturing, and agriculture all contribute to Mexico's **economy**.

Oil fields were discovered in Mexico's Gulf Coast in about 1900. The sale of oil, **petroleum**, and natural gas make up a large part of Mexico's economy.

The sale of **minerals** makes up another part of the Mexican economy. Mexico is the world's leading producer of silver. And more than forty other minerals are taken from the land and sold.

An oil refinery worker

Manufacturing products is another valuable part of the economy. Most manufacturing is done in factories in large cities. People assemble cars, make **electronics** and goods for the home, and produce iron and steel.

Tourism has grown quickly in Mexico since the 1960s. The warm climate, low prices, and new hotels and airports draw many visitors. This **industry** has created many jobs for Mexicans.

Mexicans also farm the land. Coffee, **sugarcane**, corn, **cacao**, and cotton are some of Mexico's most valuable crops. Mexicans also raise cattle and catch fish.

Although Mexico's **economy** is improving, it still has many problems. The country has more people than jobs. Many people must move from **rural** areas to cities to find work. Others must move to the U.S. to find jobs.

Because of America's **immigration** laws, some Mexicans must enter the U.S. illegally. They are forced to take low-paying jobs that require hard work.

Some Mexicans risk their lives entering the U.S. illegally by crossing the Río Grande on homemade rafts.

City Life

Mexico City is located in south-central Mexico. It is Mexico's capital, and it is the world's largest city. More than 20 million people live in Mexico City and its surrounding area.

The Spaniards built Mexico City on top of the Aztec's capital city, Tenochtitlán. Today, the city is a mix of old Aztec structures, colonial Spanish buildings, and modern skyscrapers.

Mexico City is home to the world's largest bullring, Plaza México. And it has **Latin America**'s largest church, the Metropolitan Cathedral.

Chapultepec Park is Mexico City's largest park. It has museums, a zoo, gardens, an amusement park, lakes, and fountains.

The city is also home to the National Museum of Anthropology. It teaches visitors about Mexico's Indian history and culture.

Mexico City's skyline

Mexico City's main **industries** are construction, **tourism**, and manufacturing. But industry, automobiles, and the large population have polluted the city's air. The air pollution is trapped by the surrounding mountains.

Guadalajara is Mexico's second-largest city. It is located in west-central Mexico and is the capital of Jalisco state. Guadalajara is an important industrial center. It produces soft drinks, shoes, and chemicals. And it is a valuable trading center, especially for agriculture.

Monterrey is located in northwestern Mexico. It is Mexico's third-largest city and the capital of Nuevo León state. The Pan-American Highway connects Monterrey to Laredo, Texas. This highway helped the city grow.

Monterrey is well known for its iron and steel plants. And it has some of **Latin America**'s most modern industrial structures.

Mexico City's Plaza of the Three Cultures has Aztec ruins, a colonial church, and modern buildings.

Getting Around

Trains, airplanes, and cars are the main ways to move people and goods in Mexico.

The government owns Mexico's railroads. They carry many people and goods across the country. But railway travel is not always dependable. And it can be very slow.

Flying is also an important way to travel in Mexico. The increase in **tourism** has provided Mexico with new airports and airlines.

In very **rural** areas, some Mexicans still use animals to carry goods. They use mules, donkeys, burros, and horses.

A young salesman uses a donkey to haul his firewood to market.

In Mexico City, people can ride a subway called the Metro. It is one of the busiest subways in the world. It does not cost much to ride, and it has stops all over the city.

By far, the most common way to travel in Mexico is by car. All of the main roads in the country lead to Mexico City. The Pan-American Highway stretches from Guatemala through Mexico to Laredo, Texas. It connects the Americas.

Since so many people travel by car, traffic in Mexico City is often very heavy.

The United Mexican States

Mexico's official name is the United Mexican States. The country is made up of 31 states. It also has the Federal District, where the government is located.

The Mexican government is a federal republic. This means the people elect a central government to rule the entire country.

The government follows the **Constitution** of 1917. It establishes the country's **economy** and its political system. And it promises Mexicans freedom and **civil liberties**.

The president's office is in Mexico City's Palacio Nacional.

The Constitution of 1917 divides the government's power between the president, the Congress, and the Supreme Court of Justice. All three groups are supposed to have equal power. But in truth, the president has the most power. The president serves six years and cannot be re-elected.

The Mexican people elect the president. Mexico has one main political party. It is called the Institutional Revolutionary Party (PRI). PRI has never lost a major election. PRI's major rival is the National Action Party (PAN).

Mexico's flag is green, white, and red. Green stands for independence, white for religion, and red for union among the states. In the flag's center is the Mexican coat of arms.

The Mexican coat of arms has an eagle eating a snake while sitting on a cactus. According to Aztec history, they built the city of Tenochtitlán where they saw this image.

Mexico's money is called the peso. Pesos can be broken down into smaller units called *centavos*.

Any Mexican over age eighteen may vote.

The smallest Mexican bill is worth 20 pesos.

Fiestas

In Mexico City, people celebrate Independence Day in the Zócalo Plaza.

Mexico is a land that celebrates many fiestas. Fiestas are festivals and holidays. Mexicans celebrate national, religious, and personal fiestas.

Mexico's Independence Day is on the sixteenth of September. It marks Mexico's independence from Spain. To celebrate, people gather at midnight on the fifteenth and watch fireworks. They yell "¡Viva México!" This means "Long Live Mexico!"

Mexicans also celebrate Cinco de Mayo. It is on the fifth of May. It honors the Battle of Puebla. This battle marks Mexico's independence from France.

Just before **Lent**, Mexicans celebrate Carnival. It is a time of feasting and celebrating. People watch fireworks, attend bullfights, wear masks, listen to music, and dance.

Children dress in costumes to celebrate Carnival.

On November 2, Mexicans celebrate Day of the Dead. This is a day when people honor their relatives who have died. People clean and decorate their relatives' graves with flowers and candles.

Below: Mexican girls wear traditional dresses as they dance in an Independence Day parade.

Above: A family has decorated this grave with flowers and candles for Day of the Dead.

Below: Girls dress up in brightly colored costumes to celebrate Cinco de Mayo.

Right: On Day of the Dead, Mexican children like to eat candy skulls.

Some Mexicans travel hundreds of miles to reach the Virgin of Guadalupe's church on Guadalupe Day.

Mexicans celebrate Guadalupe Day on December 12. The Virgin of Guadalupe is Mexico's **patron saint**. She is not like European saints because she has dark skin. She has become an image of Mexican identity. On Guadalupe Day, Mexicans honor the virgin at her church near Mexico City.

In the weeks before Christmas, posadas are held. Posadas retell the story of Mary and Joseph's journey in Bethlehem.

Children carry candles and dress up like Mary, Joseph, and the shepherds. They travel from house to house asking if there is room at the inn. The owners always tell them there is no room.

A Mexican child dresses as a shepherd and carries a candle for a posada.

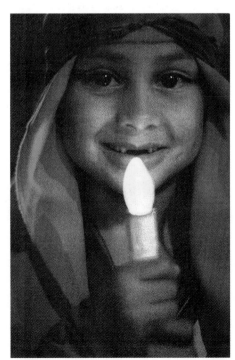

Finally, the owners of the last house they visit tell them there is room. They let the children inside and everyone celebrates. The children end the night by breaking a **piñata** that looks like the star of Bethlehem.

Another Mexican fiesta is called a *quinceañera*. It is a fiesta that celebrates a girl's fifteenth birthday. It marks her **passage** from child to adult.

The birthday girl wears a long, fancy dress. Then she goes to church. Her family and friends join her there, and a priest celebrates **mass**.

A girl from the Yucatán Peninsula blows out the candles on her quinceañera cake.

After church, most girls have a party for their family and friends. The party has dancing, music, food, and a large cake.

Mexican Culture

Mexico's most famous kind of art is the mural. Murals are large paintings that can cover the entire wall of a building. Diego Rivera, David Alfaro Siqueiros, and Jose Clemente Orozco are famous Mexican mural painters. Their murals show scenes from Mexico's history.

Handmade crafts are created throughout Mexico. Pottery and brightly-colored blankets, shawls, and baskets are popular. These items are usually sold in a town market.

A young Mariachi player

Mariachi is a popular kind of Mexican music. It began in the state of Jalisco in the 1800s. Mariachi musicians sing while they walk around playing guitars, violins, and horns. Often mariachi musicians wear decorated suits and large hats, called sombreros.

Mexicans also enjoy listening to norteño music. It began in northern Mexico and has become popular throughout the country. Norteño musicians play accordions, guitars, and drums. They sing songs about real people and their problems. Other types of music such as ranchera, salsa, cumbia, pop, and rock are also popular in Mexico.

The Palace of Fine Arts in Mexico City is home to some of Mexico's best performing arts. The National Opera, National Symphony Orchestra, and National theater perform there. Mexico's Ballet Folklórico performs at the Palace of Fine Arts, too.

Mexico's national sport is bullfighting. A bull is let into a stadium called a bullring. A person called a matador tries to kill the bull. The matador uses a cape to capture the bull's attention. As the bull draws near, the matador stabs it with a sharp sword. Some people think bullfighting is cruel. Other people admire the matador's bravery and talent.

Mexicans also enjoy soccer, baseball, and boxing. Soccer is Mexico's most popular sport. But baseball's popularity is growing. Boxing has also gained fans in Mexico.

Mexico's sports, art, and music reflect the country's unique history. The land that was once home to ancient societies and Spanish explorers has grown into a modern Mexican nation.

A bullfight in Mexico City

Glossary

cacao - a bean used to make chocolate and cocoa.

civil liberties - a person's freedom to enjoy his or her rights under the constitution.

constitution - a paper that describes a country's laws and government.

dormant - not active.

earthquake - a trembling or shaking of the ground.

economy - the way a country uses its money, goods, and natural resources.

electronics - devices that use electricity, such as radios, televisions, and computers.

fern - a kind of plant that has feathery leaves.

immigration - entry into a foreign country to live.

industry - the production of a large number of goods by business and factories.

Latin America - the region including Mexico, Central America, South America, and the West Indies.

Lent - the forty days before Easter.

mass - a worship ceremony in the Catholic Church.

mineral - a natural element, such as gold or silver, that is not of plant or animal origin.

mining - the act of removing minerals from the earth.

passage - the act of advancing or progressing.

patron saint - a saint believed to be the special protector of a church, city, state, or country.

peninsula - land that sticks out into water and is connected to a larger land mass.

petroleum - thick, yellowish-black oil that occurs naturally below the earth's surface.

piñata - a treat-filled pot made of paper. It hangs above children's heads. Children wear blindfolds and use a stick to hit the piñata until it breaks and the treats fall out.

plateau - an area of flat land.

reef - a ridge of sand, rock, or coral that lies near the surface of a sea or ocean.

reform - to make something better by getting rid of its faults.

revolution - a sudden and complete change in government.

rural - out in the country, not in the city.

scrub plants - low, small trees and shrubs.

succulent - a desert plant with a thick, juicy stem.

sugarcane - a tall grass with a thick stem from which sugar is produced.

technical - of or relating to a kind of art, science, profession, or other field.

tourism - touring or traveling for pleasure. A person traveling for pleasure is called a tourist.

traditional - something that has been passed down through generations.

union - a group of workers joined together to protect their rights.

World War II - 1939-1945, fought in Europe, Asia, and Africa. The United States, France, Great Britain, the Soviet Union, and their allies were on one side. Germany, Italy, Japan, and their allies were on the other side. The war began when Germany invaded Poland. America entered the war in 1941 after Japan bombed Pearl Harbor, Hawaii.

Web Sites

Consulate General of Mexico in New York
http://www.quicklink.com/mexico/ingles/inmain.html
This site offers information on Mexico's government, economy, and institutions. It also features a special kids section with music, games, tales, history, government, and news.

Mexico: A Country Study
http://lcweb2.loc.gov/frd/cs/mxtoc.html
The Library of Congress sponsors this site on Mexico. It has exhaustive information on Mexico's history, society, economy, government and politics, and military.

CIA: The World Factbook 1999 — Mexico
http://www.odci.gov/cia/publications/factbook/mx.html
This site by the CIA offers up-to-date statistics on Mexico. It has sections on Mexico's geography, people, government, economy, communications, transportation, military, and transnational issues.

These sites are subject to change. Go to your favorite search engine and type in "Mexico" for more sites.

Index